CW00747364

Crossings

Crossings
Gwyn Parry

Salmonpoetry

Published in 1998 by
Salmon Publishing Ltd,
Cliffs of Moher, Co. Clare

A catalogue record for this book is available from the British Library.

The Arts Council   Salmon Publishing gratefully acknowledges the
An Chomhairle Ealaíon   financial assistance of The Arts Council.

ISBN 1 897648 35 9 Softcover

Cover design by Brenda Dermody of Estresso
Cover artwork by Austin Carey
Set by Siobhán Hutson
Printed by Betaprint, Clonshaugh, Dublin 17

Er Côf Am Fy Nhad

(in memory of my father)

Acknowledgements

Some of the poems in this collection have previously appeared in *Planet Magazine*, *Poetry Ireland*, *Poetry Wales*, *Acorn*, *The Connaught Tribune*, *Copacetic*, and have been broadcast on BBC Radio 3.

Other Books by Gwyn Parry

Mynydd Parys (Seren Books, 1990)
The Hurricane (Poetry Wales Press, 1988)

Contents

Between Lands

Ship moves smooth
like sun floating morning
on steep mountain fields.

Air pegged by stone walls
shaped blue sculpture.
In the purple cloud shadow,
the small white stars
of my father's favourite flowers.

The ferry ploughs gallons
of wreck-green sea
propeller shadow-thumps
the sandy bed.

Leaving land
my astronaut suit is steel, rivet and paint.
I take a thread
tie it to the last red lighthouse,
take it across the waves
thread it through wingtips and raindrops,
leave a loose knot
on an eye-brow of island.

The Ship

Light wipes my forehead
a clean white cloth.

Light threads through me
like a needle.

I watch the lighthouse probe the cliffs,
nesting birds squint at the beam,
cormorants crucified on ledges
by the prison-break light.

The Skerries wink
between water and land,
the sea heals quietly behind us.

The Frozen Lake

The cloud leaves me naked,
a stone above the frozen lake.

Ice peels rings of blue and green,
a grey brain of water,

red deer move
through this lace of snow.

I climb down   tip-toe
the wet edges of my future.

Leaving

Within minutes
you are tilting sunlight
above the Irish Sea.
Your plane
a small cross on the sky.

Last night
I held the kite
of your neck bones

I made a print
in the smooth snow
of your skin.

Crossing

Boat cuts
the blackboard bay.

I am in your hand,
safe in your warm breath,
the scent of your hair.

I leave
beyond the white hand-rail,
push my face
into the mask of night.

At this distance,
the boat no more
than a light

chalk mark
on the cold sea.

Night Sailing

Lighthouse slaps
     this cheek
bird white light

slaps my face
     with pulse
and brilliance.

Moon mercury
licks horizon

fishing boats stammer

     two red lamps
     and a green

oil
and ultramarine.

Cliff

Under this limestone lip
Atlantic blooms, bursts
into turquoise.

This island is cut-throat
weather.
A tilting stone liner.

Wind scabs at my face,
I body-hug the Earth.

Inches
from the rest of my life,

a few glistening seconds
before the sea rushes in.

Leaving

Kissing
her shoulder bones
I think of Llyn,
its green tent of mountains
hanging on a belt
of blue sky.

Moving my head
to the hollow
between neck
and shoulder

for she has ferried me home
on her soft skin,
leaving me
to look west
at sunset.

Llyn – Llyn Peninsula

She - scape

Sun never
on her skin,
just the paw
of moonlight.
Chalk hills
she was carved,
cool limestone
her breasts.

On a road
paved with stars,
we join,
follow the hair-line
moon.
With coats of darkness
we walk
high above the sea,
our heels
studded with lighthouses.

Like that road
snaking
the headland,
I will follow
your coastline
with hands
and tongue.

I will sing you,
chant you,
bathe
in your
blue pools.

Statue

Startled by Jesus
crucified on this salty Calvary,
his two white women
weeping at his feet.

Even in this gale
he cannot feel the cold,
he cannot hear the rumble
and boom of Atlantic.

Stars fall around us
as Jesus and I smash
through the storm,
spray fizzing on our bodies
from a large wave
pounding
the darkness below.

Achill Island

Everything around,
rotting brown,
the best taken,
burnt
on a simple hearth.

The wind wraps
its razor-wire
close to the skin –
the message of this place.

Lift a stone,
find nothing
but the black
sipping bog.

Bones stained
with the land's
nicotine.

Sky brings down
a fat grey gut,
smothering the living
in a swear of weather.

Women watch
their men
open the earth,
to find
puss-filled
potatoes,
and the future
derelict
on the hillside.

Full Moon Over The Forum

The moon
our lantern tonight
hanging its warm eye
on a hook of space;
The Forum, calcium
dust orange brick.

Triumphant arches
erected in praise
or memory;
fanfares still ringing
from the green of The Palatine.

Arm in arm
we walk through Michelangelo,
down uneven steps
through centuries
of blanket-hot skies.

We stop at The Temple of Saturn;
the arthritic columns
of The Temple of Jupiter.

From our silent vantage point
we feel and listen,
hear the slow crumbling of Empire
the thrust of traffic
round The Coloseum.

Cuevas de la Piletas

Poppies flick their heads
in the solar drench,
mountains outstare us.

With hissing paraffin lamps
we enter the cave.
Bats cog-wheel on the cavern roof,
stalagmites piston in front.

There are animals,
bison, deer, birds.
Battles, weddings, births.
25,000 years
in ochre and charcoal
deep in this mountain sketch-book.

A buffalo, stickman
throws his arrow,
a fish,
left dry on the rock.

Lindow Man

My face is
cheek to cheek
    with his.
We examine each other;
my eyes
    his,
my stubble
    his neat-cut beard
my blood
    his.
He lies on his side,
half-asleep bronze,

his ear
leather butter-curl,

his lips
    so thirsty.

Lindow Man's stomach
writhes like water
in this shallow glass pool,

he tries to get up
step out and back.

I watch his face,
the despair of a young man.

He cannot move now,
not even to shade his eyes,

he is spot-lit
in time's endless room.

*Lindow Man was ritually sacrificed
to the celtic gods 2000 years ago.*

Earth Calling

On Sirius
they are following
the first episodes
of Coronation Street.

Somewhere
in the Square of Pegasus
Hawaii 5-0
makes little sense.

On Venus
reception is poor
but Dallas glamour
seeps through
only to flounder
in the acid oceans.

Beyond the galaxy
our signals
bounce off never
lit moons,

Important
news bulletins
inform
million-mile
dust storms.

Eclipse

Tonight,
mothers, fathers,
children, lovers,
stand
in a half-lit world.

Motorways stop,
trains rest at their buffers,
ships sleep snug
in their docks.

Like time pieces,
sundial still,
we watch
through thin cloud
the Earth
weeping
across the face
of the moon.

San Andrea

A place where cats
purr away the night,
the courtyard open
to May downpours.

In our room,
the window
lets the thunder in,
rain lashing
small towns
riding
the green hills below.

In our vaulted room
a table, sink
and simple bed,
years of prayer
binding the building
together,
solitary souls
made calm
this world.

In our room,
plain, white-washed,
a view of a cross
and terracotta roof –
we let the silence
build
between us.

Cave

This cave is ink.
I go and bend my head
in respect.
Legs are alcoholic,
the ground swimming
up and down.

Bent double
hands on the floor,
an animal.

I think my eyes are open,
there is sick in my throat
and a thump of sea.

Turning back,
eyes crash on light,
I walk slowly
upright.

Fish in the Tolka

I watch fish
writhe a stinking
iron-current river.

Water solid
scale and fin,
battalions, armour.

Rubbing each other,
pouting, pouting.

A swan crosses
this living oil-slick,
too white
for this scene.

Sometimes,
as a train slurs past,
the fish flick
their thousand tails.

Kilronan Harbour

Dead fish
in clear clear water,
their sides
mercury.

Silver saws
from a child's tool box.
The fish lie scattered,
new shiny nails.

The largest fish
has a cigarette-long snout,
its eye a brooch of blood.

Quarry Divers

They step off the land
and fall through centuries.
They are searching deep
in this death-water.

Some find it
in half-collapsed tunnels,
others follow black railways
until there is no further.

Here in this sunless station
they find it,
lit by sick-yellow
torchlight.

Their throats blocked
by slate-blue water.

Mining

Trees at night
are cracks in the sky,
canyons where I pot-hole
between blankets of stars.

In the deepest fissure
I come across miners
their candles half-used,
their tools dripping with light.

They are working
God's dark vein.

The Voyage

Leaving the calm
of the harbour
we enter
the palm
of the Atlantic,
our boat
a pendulum.

The island
tilts
on the horizon;
night
drowns the world.

On deck
with a dog
and a local,
I hold
the ladder-rail,
while the deep
blooms
over my feet.

Our ferry
makes the mainland,
with no more
than sick stomachs
and dizzy heads.

But
on that heave
of ocean,
I understood,
how we all are
small boats
thrown
from feeling
to feeling,
our captains
hard at the wheel.

And how unlike ferries
that link
rock
to rock
we are,

our hearts
making
for the horizon,
searching
the deep troughs
of uncharted waters.

New Year's Day

Her bus reaches Kinnegad,
my ship leaves the smile
of Dublin Bay.

I watch gulls dip for fish,
Howth not close enough to swim.

On this new year's day
I force myself to sleep,
and catch-up with her bus in Moate,
buy my ticket off the driver.

I sit next to her
for the rest of the way.

Flight

The cigar of your plane
takes off, skews
towards where I'm waiting.

I stand by the blue runway
of the Royal Canal,
the jet's fat belly
silvers above me.

With all my powers
I pull you down
out of your seat,
hug you
one last time

then let you go
skipping,
into a long hall-way
of sunlight.

Wood Carving

Her father chose
a perfect piece of wood
and carved
for her mother,
making sure the shapes
were good and strong,
smoothing and rounding
the best he could.
He carved
a beautiful daughter.
Her insides he made
intricate as a small town,
roads leading to the heart
where he chiselled-out
a place for himself.

I thank your father
for his skill
and eye for detail,
and for the way
he sculptured
you.

New Year

I stand on the year's turning,
a shadow on the seal-grey sea.

I am a hole in prismed light,
a watermark on the knife tide.

Light falls as quiet as snow,
fans the forest sea.

From back door to threshold
there is only the wind's cold song
and the road's pitching darkness.

Moonchild

Between my father and mother
I straggle my arms,
swing
in their warm gloved hands
bathing my face
in the ballooning moon.

The road takes us
beneath its skirts of darkness
to the pin-glitter of sea,
to a curve in the road
where the river mists breath,
letting our shadows
run away with the stream.

Tonight
on the road alone,
the moon moves
in a feather-touch of clouds,
takes me along
to nights of Sunday stillness
dogs barking on frost covered farms,
trees creaking their anchors
blue night winds
soft-filling their sails.

In Dreams

I am taken skywards
until the earth is line
and colour of maps,
the sea a chart
of fading blue.

From free-fall
I watch mountains lean
their shadow pyramids
walking the bowed plains
in long evening light.
Lakes
frozen badges
on winter's dark cloth.

From this great height
I see a child
running through a field
of wet wheat,
clothes soaking the rain,
the wool of his jumper
heavy.

The same child
warms his face
close to an October bonfire,
knowing how delicate
his young skin,
understanding
fires lit
on special nights,
the aluminium of moonlight,
the bend of trees
ash-white
on autumn skies.

World

My world at eight –
down the yard
to the gate,
where mam
beat the carpet.

The graveyard,
tall grass
where the evening
left the cage
of an old farm
on the horizon.

The tongue-poke
of sea
blue beaten
by clouds
and red tankers
on their way to Liverpool.

To the north
the land rose
in a wave of rooks,
oaks and chestnuts
where we conkered
every autumn –
me pointing
out the fat ones.

In the south
Bodafon hill,
where I flew my kite
with white string,
saw the island
green – stitched.

At night,
mam and dad in bed,
I'd open my window,
hang my legs out
to the sounds of owls
the tall cries of foxes.

Head up 'till it hurt,
I saw heaven,
drank the stars
the floss
of the Milky Way,
my lungs filling
with deep space.

The Shark

It took the two of us
three whole days
to make the shark.
With our minds
we plumbed the depths
of blue,
diving beyond
the paper and picture books
of coral reefs and submarines.

From the sandy bed
we coloured upwards
with pastels
and green paint.
Halfway
we found the outline
waiting
to be coloured in.

You took charge of the fins and gills,
I made the thick grey and brown
rubbed the body smooth to swim.
The white teeth
put in like a sharp saw,
his grin.

Months
the shark swam
on the school wall.

In assemblies,
during hymns
and The Lord's Prayer
I would dive,
air tanks and all,
float
along thousand foot chasms,
the wrecks of ships
falling around me,
and always
between me and the sky,
the dark plough
of the shark.

Red

It is red
and flows like a stream.

I watch it wrap
around trees,
stringing in the branches,
red tattered limbs.

In the morning it will rise,
pour over the hills,

smooth itself
round the corners of houses.

At Fron Ddrain
the bees suffer in the scarlet light,

it glares through the gate
it slides into the hives.

Children let it into their mouths
without knowing,
chewing it as they speak.

On strong nights full of breathless stars
clouds clot red in the sky,

through the gap in the door
I see its red smile

from my bed
I see it smudge crimson on the window.

Barber

Three miles walk for a hair-cut,
dad's tongue, whip-like
telling me I'm not tired,
that it isn't much further.

Wil Pendre's hut is held together
with not quite knocked-in-nails
and old Exide battery signs.
I sit on a bum-smooth bench
with tobacco-stained old men.

My turn,
I perch on a plank
across the barber's high chair,
eye to eye with Wil.
He knows only one style –
desert campaign, 1944,
Africa.
His big hands on my young neck,
his face so close
I get the alcohol off his breath.

I sit like a brush.
Wil has no time for children,
he prefers the heat,
the sand gritting his scissors,
his favourite salon
a well camouflaged tank.

My fringe cut as crooked as possible,
my neck shaved like a pine cone,
I am walked home,
ear lobes
slightly bleeding.

Fron Ddrain

Fordson Bach

Sheet-zinc doors
with a gap for a boy,
dark world of spanners
and biting vices,
steel bars, pliers,
monkey wrenches.

The tractor stands
like a horse.
It lives here
with paraffin cans
saws and axes,
the scent of wood shavings.

'More paraffin, Gwyn,
pull the throttle,
don't touch the gears'.

Belching black
on the tin roof,
noise echoes for miles.

I open
and close the gate,
duck under branches,
follow last years tracks.

Ty'n Buarth, Pandy, Afon Goch
all were singing
with sky and sun,
you drove
while I counted smoke rings.

Collecting Stones

A flat field,
the flattest in Anglesey.
We bend into sickle-shapes
lifting stones,
stacking them like sculls
on the front of the trailer.
Nothing but white stones.

String

I pull the horsetail
of bailer-twine
hanging in the dust-light.

Knots like adams apples
between my fingers,
fronds float
in the warm air.

Your clogs clack
on the stone floor.
You show me knots
for tying straw,
knots to hold the summer.

Bee Keeping

Books full of honeycombs
and about the queen's habits
and how the workers loved her.

You teach me bee-words,
Apis Melifera,
magnifying glass enlarging
for your dim eyes.

I make the bee food,
       just right,
Two pounds of sugar
to a pint of water,
stir with a warm spoon.

In the garden they hum,
landing with heather
from Mynydd Bodafon,
sea-pink from Dulas,
the air hot with drone.

Inside the hive
they dance
a sun dance,
build their miracle shapes.

Er cof am Huw Owen, Fron Ddrain.

Kite

It would take a week
to persuade my father
to make a kite.

On Saturday
he would suddenly say,
find a broken umbrella,
coarse twine, newspaper,
a straight branch of willow
or beading
from an old chest-of-drawers.

Then
mix flour and water
into a sticky paste.
The balance
just right,
my father bent
umbrella steel,
a tense arc
over a thin
cross of wood.

Local newspapers
we'd paste taut
on the coffin shape
joining centre-spreads
together.

The sun dried our kite
while I plaited a tail
of bailer-twine,
dickie-bows of newsprint.

The wind, my father said,
would come from the west,
licking his finger
to test the air.

Harness complete
we laid out the kite in a field,
tail long as a girl's hair.
Dad held the kite above his head
and I ran with the line
arm straining
at the pull of the wind.

It was climbing
string thrumming,
burning
letting-out
through my soft hands.

With my father
I watched
as headlines
became foot-notes,
the kite
a small shimmering doorway
on a patch of sky.

Lake

The whistle of wind
rain black-handing
down from the mountain.
In the quarries
water fingers its perimeter,
rising cold arctic.

Trees single root
sore unrelenting slate.
I live alone
watching for horizons.
I have no inside
no outside,
but am somewhere
in childhood,
sharing my mother's bed,
hay-making,
beach-walking;
the warm hand
of my father.

In the mountains
above the stubble of slate
there is a staircase
of white water,
each step brings me closer
to the black of a corrie lake,
to a sharp
shelving
shore.

Boy

Reaching the white rocks
seaweed turns into deep sea.
I can feel the thudding
engines of ships
balancing on the horizon.
I find a moon of sand
cupped between barnacled rocks,
a place to sit
on an ebbing tide.
Seals cry
a mile off-shore,
their lives rocking
rocking.

Sitting between land and tide
I watch dad rasp his hook
down throats of rock.
Sun setting
the red of my heart,
sea pushes me
from the glitter of evening,
pushes me
to my father's salty arms
to his warm coat
and the starry walk home.

Ditch Digging

Four fields and a copse to cut,
every Saturday knee-deep in mud.
I take dad his dinner –
bara menyn a te.

I watch him from a distance,
body-scalpel in a ditch.
He eats his bread
drinks his tea.

There is no breeze or cloud-shadow
just the singing of blue air
and the warm shade
of a mid-day wall.

bara menyn a te – bread and butter and tea

Snow Clearing

When the snow came
dad left at four in the morning.
The night all yellow
with JCB lights,
the smell of oil-skins.
The land white as a mountain hare,
the hills softened to a whisper.

Moses

Leads traffic.
The junction in front of his closed shop
next to the post office is his.
He works better with tourists
for they believe in him.
Locals just indicate left
then turn right.

He's directed them all,
seen models change
from Austin to Vauxhall,
Japanese.

Late at night
when the traffic stops
he guides the invisible.
He handles the souls of vehicles,
nightmare lorries that shake our sleep,
buses of ashen-faced children,
un-lit, engine-less cars.
Moses leads them
with the width of his hand.

Mechanics

Ted 'Ceir'

Ted sat at the table
after fixing dad's car.
Sump-black hands
he held the red tomato tight,
smearing it with castrol.
Mother gave him a cloth,
he refused
and ate the tomato.

Ted was a real mechanic,
every bristle and blackhead
oozed oil,
each pore and wrinkle
sweating the black stuff.

Ted lived with chickens and goats
in a broken-back roofed house
on a sharp bend in the road.
Ted said it was handy.

Dan 'Storws'

Dan lived by the estuary
with the call of Oystercatchers
and Curlews.
On summer evenings he'd be under Jaguars
or maybe a green Daimler,
his face war-paint clutch fluid.

Dan knew a fault by the noise,
or lack of noise.
He lived engines
and fine tuning,
his music was cat-purr
smooth running.

Mike's Dad

Mints flew across the dashboard,
I faced the way I came from,
stopped an inch from the lamp post.

My wheel came off on New Year's Eve
on a by-pass.
I thought of Mike's dad and his JCB.

I arrived in the middle of Out of Africa.
Zebras tore across the screen, then he said,
'let's go.'

I've rescued women in Morris Minors,
I've pulled preachers from hedges
and drunks from ditches.

There's nothing I like better
than a good rescue,
besides
I'd seen that film before.

McGuire

A red dashboard light
and rain enough to drown
water drilling roads,
the wettest day of November.
A week after my father's funeral
I sit dripping in my brother's kitchen.

The tow-rope snaps and cracks
on the wet bends,
my breath smudging countryside
on the cold windscreen.

Maguire stands in the yawn
of his garage door.
Unshaven
profile sharp as a cleaver.

He goes straight for compression,
the engine coughs.

'The car isn't worth it.
By the way,
sorry to hear about your father,
I didn't know.'

Psychic Mechanic

He warns us to step back from the car.
The psychic mechanic,
no need to oil his hands
or wrestle with a heat-fused nut.
Mind over machine
he probes and illuminates.

Starting up
he smashes wall-to-wall
February fog,
spears the car
through this overcoat of night.

There is no charge,
for this is his vocation
machine, doctor,
bone-setter.

He hands back the car keys
ignition switch
fixed.

Scrap

Evans' face glows like a lamp
in the minus cold,
his nose a thriving exotic fungi.
I need a light switch
for an S reg. Marina,
he takes me to the shed.

Shelves of insect antennae,
proboscis dangling limp,
walls crawl with whole switch-units,
extracted from every long-gone model
heaped like lobsters.

'You're lucky –
it's a tenner,
should be fifty.'

Outside
the sun heads for mid-December,
the light bowling low
across the frozen fields.
I start the car,
leave the carnage
of his scrap-yard.

Dead Men

Whaler

I am a whaler,
cut them open
to the waxy inside.
I sailed past Fjords
to the always day.
Followed Krill
to the edge of ice.
I smell of sweet
sperm-oil.

Soldier

I lost my arm
to a sword at Ypres,
came home
to my dead wife,
raised my boys
single-handed.
Two, they say,
became lawyers –
did well.

Gwâs

I work on farms,
do the harvest,
planting, ditch-digging.
I get meals and a roof.
Gwâs Bach they call me,
I sleep in the out-houses.

Labourer

The roads
is what I do,
up at six for the lorry.
Winter gives me foot-rot,
chilblains the size of marbles.
At lunch time
we play poker,
bet cigarettes and matches.

Sailor

Blush Rose,
the name of my ship.
Sailed her
back and forth,
scrap, old iron
for the smelter.

Slung in a camp I was
all through the war.
I ate rats and vegetables.
It was always cold.

Poet

Writing,
that's all I do.
Versus and sonnets,
no rhyme at all
sometimes.
I had a book or two,
people said I was good,
but that
was a long time ago.

Roadkill

I kneel next to your face,
you stretch like a cat
warm on tarmac.

I listen for a breath
or word
from your folded face.

Your mother will hold you
close like a baby,
repeating, repeating
your name.

She will clean wounds,
wipe dirt and blood
from your eyes.
Your mother will cradle
your broken head.
She will fix your checkshirt,
collect your shoes off the road.

I sit with you
until the ambulance blues our skin.
I let them hammer on your heart,
I let them kiss you.

I tell the police
I met you
lying across my lights,
and how we camped out
on this dark night.

Sunday Night Walking

Holding hands
we go universe walking,
moon at the crick of my neck,
milky way across my forehead.
Lace of stars wash my face,
breath of radio
the rocking pulse
and gentle tilt of Earth.

Conducting

Conducting the world's orchestras
with a knitting needle
in front of the red dresser.
I made it look easy
oratorios, sonatas, symphonies
all with my mother's number 8 needle.
In the quiet pieces
I bent in half, my hand steady
steadying, bringing the next solo in.

My father didn't mind,
my conducting was silent.
Sunday nights after chapel
I danced to the minute waltz,
my dad closed his eyes through Chopin.

Funerals

Men in the graveyard
in long grey greatcoats,
steaming in the drizzle
like cattle.

There was no colour
on funeral days,
my mother drew the curtains,
leaving us wrapped up
in brown-parcel light.

In the graveyard
the men went on standing,
red clay
on their black turn-ups.
The women are outriders
to this sullen crowd,
their tiny, shiny heels
sink in the mud.

Pneumonia

My father's weight
rests on my arms.
I hold his body
close to my heart,
his mind warm and silent
in my pocket.

I hand him over
like a paper bag,
his white hair
feather in the breeze.

My mother holds me,
puts a key in my hand.
The doors close
on the sunlit ambulance.

After the panic of engines
and blue lights,
I am left crying by an iron gate,
by a border of Sweet Williams.

Lost

He is lost
in the dark field
of his bedroom.
Illness stone-walls him.

The gate in his mind
is cold brown iron,
his strength is
not to open it.

With the light switch
bring him inside,
lift him,
float him
on the bed sheets.

My mother cries
for his white
seal-pup body.

Sleeping

at the foot
of my father's bed,
I listen to his faint breath
and the weakness in his chest.

In the night
I am a small
forgotten god
       holding
       this dark world
from the next.

Ferry

My father leans out of the hot car,
a draught messing his hair.

Not strong enough to stand,
he dangles his legs off the seat
like a child.

My mother waves from the jetty,
ship pushing
the land away.

Mother flags her handkerchief,
as if it is me
who is leaving forever.

Waves

Horses of white and green
salt dusting the highest crests.
Enveloped in cream
I'm lifted, licked
taken out to sea.

Hit again, my world flips,
my face to the sea's mirror
sand shifting beneath my back.

Through the lens of water
I feel the August sun,
my body cold razor shell
caught in the twist of Atlantic.

In my dream
I stand at your hospital bed,
dark mountains of night
behind me.

You are asleep,
newspaper by your side.

Then
I see you come
body horizontal, effortless.

You slap heavy
wet and salty,
breaking through me
light and darkness.

I stand still,
your wave broken,
your bed empty.

At 2.00 a.m.
my brother wakes me
with news I know already.

The Hand

Taking a photograph
of my father,
a bird
landed on my camera.
I stayed still
in case I scared it.

Through the lens
I watched my father
incredulous, smiling
saying, don't move.
He came towards me,
his white hair
tanned skin
soft orange in the sunset.

We watched
this miracle
of yellow
and green,
the beak
a pale silver,
its eye
a tiny pool
of ink.

My father held out
his hand,
and the bird
hopped,

perching on a finger.
'It's young,' he said,
'doesn't know
not to trust.'

That evening
I took a photograph
of the baby bird
resting on my father's hand.
I focused hard
and sharp,
close-up,
exposing film
to that marigold light
the best I could.

When I take out
the picture now,
I forget
to look at the bird.

Home

Cries at his mother's breast,
home to an empty room,
his father gone.

Don't cry,
my youngest,
he would not want this.

While his mother washes,
he finds a form
in the living room,

he moves into it,
sits
in a warm tingling suit.

Mam

A sleepless night,
she has been rummaging
thoughts;
how kind my father was,
how if she wanted anything
he would say,
have it, go ahead.

Hand on her shoulder,
comfort is nothing
this dark December morning.
My voice has not the resonance
she is looking for.

Search

Looking for signs
on the kitchen table,
the mug you drank from,
the side you sat on.

I stay through winter
with my mother,
searching together,
taking the car to places
you were last seen.
Beaches, headlands
that still hold
more than a shadow.

On my own
I take to nearby fields,
re-create the time
putting firewood in bags,
dragging branches home,
to cut with your saw.

Chair

We watch the eclipse together,
the moon half-dark
above your head.
Your chair underneath the window,
we kept the curtains open
to watch moonlight
become thumbprint.

Now, your chair is in a room
you never sat in.
I warm on a different fire.
Searching the cotton-sun days
I find you sitting,
listening to the Irish station,
the warm voice of a tenor.

I sit with you at the table,
electric heater on
to bring blood to your blue-fingered hands.
You stir too much sugar into your tea,
watch horses from the window;
their coats packed with winter mud.

I was small,
watching the late football with you.
I lay on the settee 'till after eleven –
you carried me to bed,
asleep before the end of the match.

There are hundreds of days
since I saw you last,
but yesterday
I saw my brother scratch his back
and stand a certain way.
I saw myself eating soup
with your hands.

October

My father steps from the car,
his jacket too big for him,
the house step too high.

His breath tight for washing-up,
sparse for splitting fire-wood.

He lost his jobs
to his youngest son.

I miss
the white bristle
on your oak-solid neck,
the pearl-blue eyes
picking quotes from the Bible.

October,
time turns on its heel,
dark early-fire-lighting
winter evenings.

I want to sit with you by the sea
feel the rough palm of your hand.
I want to walk late summer sun.
I want to sit in car parks
the car full of roll-your-own smoke.

October,
the cold snatches
through the coat you gave me.

Three months,
I cut short the winter
with my mother,
slowly putting your things
in the big wardrobe,
except your shoes and dictionary.

A plastic bag from the hospital
marked PARRI,
your glasses, comb, wallet, toothbrush,
tobacco tin
worn hand-smooth
in your pocket.
Cold November
I scrape frost off your car,
check anti-freeze.
I saw logs,
walk the fields for dead wood.

Some days, I find you
holding the sack for me,
and I break the wood with my knee.

October again,
and we are starlight
distance.